Teaching with Argumentation
A Quick Start Guide

Jeremy S. Edge, PhD.

ISBN: 0996623426
ISBN-13: 978-0-9966234-2-1

DEDICATION

As is everything I do, this work is dedicated to the hardworking educators who make a difference each and every day.

ACKNOWLEDGMENTS

I would like to thank my colleagues and students for testing these ideas and scaffolds over the recent years. I am forever grateful to my family for understanding my need to continually get these ideas out and on paper.

Jeremy S. Edge, PhD.

Argumentation is a way of thinking. Each subject we teach, each situation we face in life, and everything in between requires thinking. Circumstances we encounter must be approached with a thought process...so...why not have a methodology that allows for the best possible outcome? For educators, the great benefit in teaching the concept of argumentation, and teaching through argumentation, is that this way of thinking is precisely what we want to see in our students. A pupil who thinks in the manner of argumentation examines information differently. When a student thinks argumentatively, they are simultaneously thinking critically and metacognitively. Teaching the concept of argumentation then allows educators to teach *through* argumentation. Together, these methods push students further than they generally go with traditional teaching methodologies.

In a previous publication, *Argumentation: Putting Argument to Work in Your Classroom*, I have thoroughly detailed the theoretical basis that supports argumentation. I also illuminated a plan for implementing argumentation in the classroom. After some thought, however, I assumed that a "quick and easy" start may help educators see how well this can work in their classrooms. In what follows, you will see basic techniques and explanations that will allow any educator to get started teaching their students the argumentative approach to thinking and learning. Thinking in an argumentative style involves students questioning the information they encounter as well as the sources. More importantly, it involves an intrinsic questioning of their approach to that information and their own thinking as well. Through argumentation, and the way in which understandings and thought processes must be examined in argumentative thinking, students understand the bias, motivations, and power structures involved within sources as well as within themselves. It is this critical assessment of whatever they encounter that will produce the thinkers and citizens of a great world.

The individual pieces of an argument each require a different approach to the subject matter at hand. Constructing an argument involves specific intellectual and philosophical techniques. Constructing the claim necessitates organizing your understanding of the subject and stating it succinctly. Deciding on the evidence that is appropriate to support the ideas you have developed requires critically assessing what you have encountered. Explaining your reasoning forces you to truly understand and lay out the thought processes and way of thinking that leads to the claim, connects the evidence to the claim, and does so thoroughly. Perhaps the most difficult part of creating a solid argument is formulating a counterclaim and rebuttal. These pieces lead the thinker to examine the evidence from different perspectives and truly think critically about the subject matter. In this quick start guide, we will look at each piece of argument and examine a scaffold for students to jump right onto developing arguments...with a little help. The argument map scaffold is a great way to visualize the argument and how the pieces fit together and flow from each other. With a picture of what our argument consists of, students can be walked through the process of argument simply and effectively with what is referred to as a socio-scientific scenario. These scenarios are often controversial, emotional, or refer to morality. I use socio-scientific topics to get students engaged and thinking. The more they are invested in the introductory lesson, the more likely they will be hooked on proving points, being right, and being more aware of the world around them. The secret is finding a topic that is both appropriate and divisive. The topic needs to have a basis in fact so students learn that

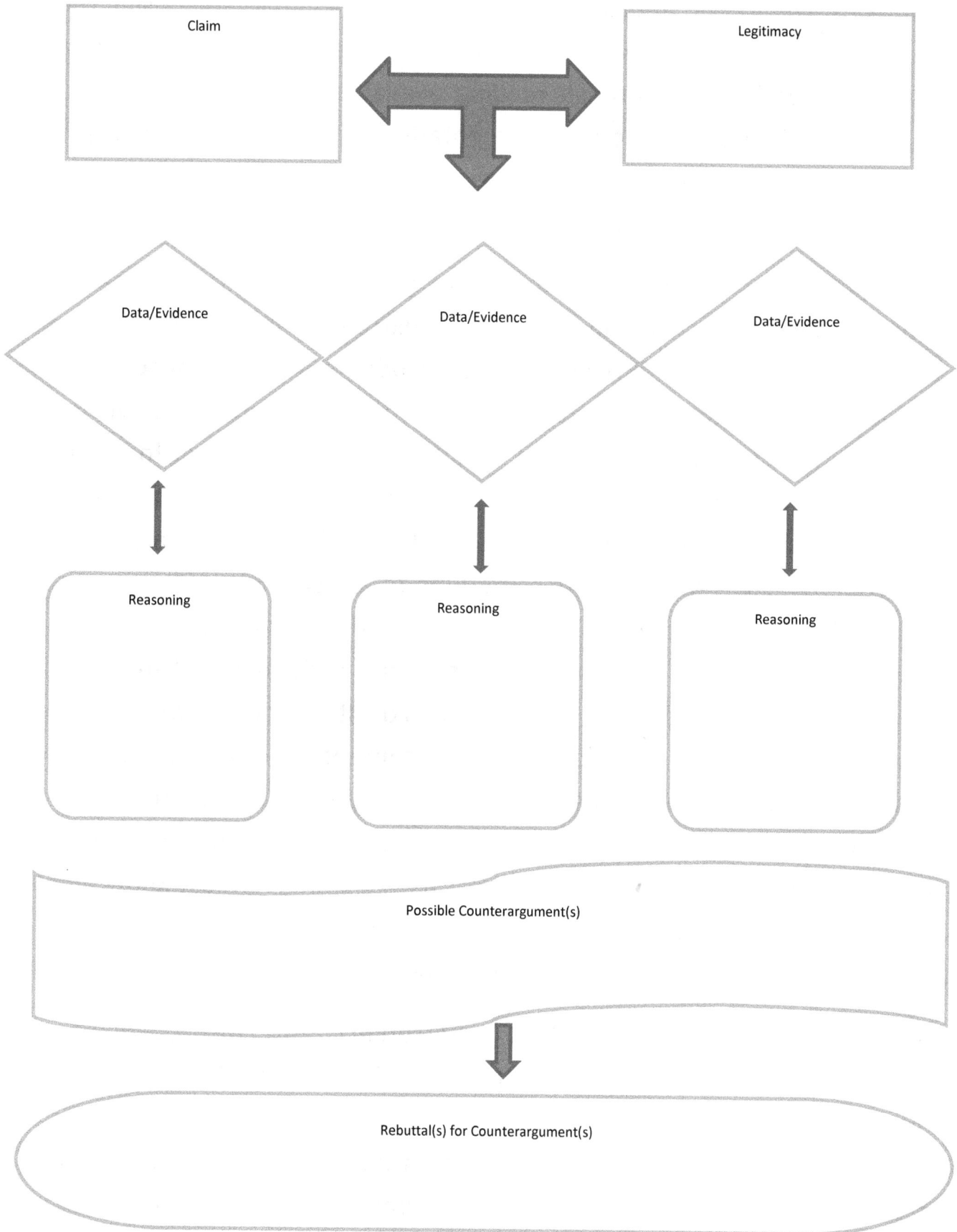

Argument Map

Claim		Legitimacy

Data/Evidence

Data/Evidence

Data/Evidence

Reasoning

Reasoning

Reasoning

Possible Counterargument(s)

Rebuttal(s) for Counterargument(s)

evidence is of utmost importance. I have used topics such as: examining the legal drinking age, iOS vs. Android, renting vs. buying a home, and raising the minimum wage. No matter what the topic of choice is, one should have a small amount of factually intense reading available that can be perused quickly. In addition, having the basic presentation of the pieces of argument ready to go through as you create an argument via classroom participation and think aloud from the teacher.

The trifecta of initiation into the art of argumentation (topic, readily available evidence, and the think aloud) is extremely important for the students' understandings. In my experience, students work best when they are immersed in the art of argumentation and then it is broken down for them rather than vice versa. The think aloud piece can be difficult for some teachers if they are not used to the experience. Students need to hear what someone who understands the process is thinking. The modeling aspect of this introduction gives the students something to attach their thinking to as they work their way through the process. For the introduction I use a streamlined presentation that also doubles as my bulletin board material. The premise is a pneumonic device to aid students in writing an argumentative essay, but also works for an argument in science, math, and social studies. The basic premises of argument are similar across curriculum areas. The most significant difference is what counts as evidence in each area...and that can be left up to the teacher to explain. You must know and understand your subject matter in order to teach students the basic epistemological beliefs of the content area in which they argue.

The pneumonic device is A-BCERCR (A Berserker). This corresponds to a legendary group of Norse warriors that had especially powerful ability. This is not really pivotal to the overall idea...but it works. Each of the letters correspond to an essential part of creating an argument. The "A" stands for "Audience." Students need to fully and deeply understand that each

A-BCERCR

A- Audience - You must balance being clear enough in your explanations with treating your audience like they know more or less than they do...

B – Background – What is the issue at hand and what do we already know about it?

C- Claim – Thesis statement – What are you trying to prove or convince others of?

E – Evidence – What FACTS or legitimate evidence do you have that support your assertions?

R – Reasoning - How do your facts support your claim? What do the connections mean and how are they made?

C – Counterargument – What is an alternative point of view or another way to interpret the facts?

R- Rebuttal – Why is the alternative not the best interpretation? Why are some of the reasons that the counterargument is based on not true or not the best way to think. Why is your idea better?

time they are working with an audience, such as when they write something to be read, debate a subject with someone, or any interaction when they are presenting information or persuading, they must cater to whom they are directing their work and for what purpose they have created that work. The first "B" is a reminder that background should be included. In an essay, the background is often included in the opening paragraph and precedes the claim (thesis) itself. In science, the background contains the understandings that one must have before an understanding of the actual controversy can be developed or the background knowledge necessary to examine observable data. Background in the sciences can also include previous experiences. In the social sciences, the background is often related to the time period, social climate, or previous experience of those involved. It is related to the history and content of the topic. Overall, the background contextualizes the topic. The first "C" represents the claim. This is the overall thesis or what is being argued. This is the point that is to be supported by evidence and reasoning. All things that come after the claim should relate to the claim in some way. The claim should be concise and specific. It is developed from the evidence and not the other way around. Although the evidence follows the stated claim in the argumentative session or writing, the evidence leads us to where we need to be. Those who think critically and assess information to derive understandings cannot purport to have those understandings without the information guiding them to those understandings. The consideration of audience, the background, and the claim give students what they need for the introduction.

The rest of our pneumonic device describes the body of the argumentative paper or the bulk of the argumentative session. The "E" represents the idea of evidence. Within each content area there is a different idea of what actually constitutes evidence, what can be used as evidence, and even what *should* be used as evidence. At the heart of this are the epistemological beliefs accepted by an academic field. Each area has at its foundation what it is they hold as knowledge and understanding. They decide what can be used as evidence and what the sources of that evidence can and should be. With the readings that the teacher has selected for the introductory activity, there should be easy-to-find evidence. Pointing out to the students the basis for the choices of readings and of the evidence necessary to come to a claim is pivotal in the beginning. This will aid students in choosing evidence that is from legitimate sources. As the teacher thinks aloud and works through finding evidence with the students, they see a first-hand account of how the trained argumentative thinker examines evidence and derives support for the claim with that evidence.

The first "R" stands for reasoning. This is one of the parts of an argument that many students leave out or struggle with. Reasoning is where the author truly presents their way of thinking in their argument. If the student does not fully relay to the audience how they connected the evidence to their claim and, more specifically, how they reasoned through those connections, then the argument falls short of its intended purpose. The idea of reasoning contains a pivotal part of any argument. Reasoning is the collection of ideas about how the thinker came to the claim and how the evidence specifically supports that claim. Students need to clearly and thoroughly connect the evidence with the claim. To do this, they should explain the way of thinking about the evidence that they followed to arrive at the claim. This involves both explaining the cited evidence and the connections while detailing how to deliberate about the ideas to get to the same conclusion. Essentially, the author of the argument should do all of the thinking for the audience. That way, there is no confusion and the audience thoroughly and clearly understands what the author is trying to convey.

The first three parts of argument are often referred to as CER, or claims-evidence-reasoning. This is often what students learn about argument. However, as we continue through the pneumonic, the second "C" represents a new level of critical thinking and assessment for students. The idea of a counterargument is one of the more difficult things for students to develop. If students are not thinking critically yet, then this piece of argumentation will drive them towards that goal. Students need to understand that the counterargument is not the opposing or opposite position. It can be, but that is not necessarily the case. I find that this is one of the more difficult ideas to convey (current research agrees) to students. Before actually deriving a counterclaim, it has likely become clear that examining evidence and devising a claim based on fact can be difficult. During the research phase of any argumentative situation or project, students should be critically examining evidence in order to distill their understandings into a claim that can be supported and hopefully makes sense to the arguer. When students develop a claim through a critical analysis of the evidence, then their claim tends to be more arguable and more enduring. Students should approach their initial research without any preconceived notions or ideas regarding the subject matter. Of course most find this to be practically impossible.

As intelligent beings, if we have background knowledge of a subject or idea, then we generally have some bias already. It is difficult to reason through that bias when creating a claim and developing an argument. However, once students reach the counterargument phase, it is necessary to truly examine the alternates that they may not have considered previously. When students practice with counterargument and the final phase of argument, rebuttal, they further develop the critical thinking and metacognitive skills that will make them better at the CER pieces of argument as well. To develop a counterargument, students examine the alternatives to their ideas. They must truthfully and honestly examine the evidence, including evidence that they did not use to support their claim, in order to determine what alternative claims could be. Essentially, they are determining what another person might argue based on the evidence. The counterargument could be considered the CER process from one or more alternate perspectives...still based in evidence, though.

The final letter, the second "R" in BCERCR, continues the critical assessment of both the original claim and the counterargument. This final phase of argument is the rebuttal. In the rebuttal, the arguer descends upon the counterargument in an attempt to disprove some piece of that claim and at the same time bolster the original claim, if possible. In order to accomplish this goal, one must examine the plausible evidence in support of the counterargument as well as the reasoning that may be attached to that evidence. The rebuttal can take the form of making a case against the appropriateness of the evidence used in support of the counterargument. The arguer can find issues with the legitimacy of the evidence itself, with the source, or with the way it is used to support the argument. In addition, one can make a case against the reasoning used to connect the evidence to the counterargument. Rebuttals can also make use of more evidence on the side of the original argument to make the original case even stronger. When there is ample evidence, some can be moved from the exposition section of the argument to the rebuttal section, especially if that bit of evidence is pivotal to the rebuttal of the ideas of the counterargument. The evidence can also merely be repeated or further expounded upon. When both methods are used in tandem, the rebuttal is stronger and more likely to refute the counterargument while simultaneously supporting the foundational points of the argument.

Perhaps the most important actual teaching a person can do is to encourage the critical examination of evidence, ideas, and conclusions while assuming the intense burden of introspection. Throughout the process of creating an argument, critical thinking and critical assessment are pivotal. With that being said, students often do not understand or respond to the idea of thinking critically about things. In my experience, learners begin the road to critical thinking more efficiently if I give them a critical thinking checklist. Each checklist can be content specific or there may be a universal checklist for all students across all content areas, depending on the needs of the school, subject area, or individual teacher. In general, though, the ideas represented for students include, but are not limited to: individual bias, informational bias, power structure and the power relationships behind ideas and information, perspective of all involved in each scenario, the legitimacy of information and ideas, to whom items are important and why, motivation of parties involved with information and actions, and most importantly, the student's preconceived notions and possible bias towards the subject matter. A checklist style of teaching critical thinking allows students to be metacognitively aware of where they are in their learning and in their ideas. With repeated use, students will internalize the checklists and add it to their mental "bag of tricks" for thinking and performing both academically and in the world outside of school. Overall, students must have the willingness to see other points of view and entertain different ideas if they are to think critically.

In my teaching, to examine something critically means to see it from multiple perspectives. The first step I take with students is to ask about and discuss the perspective opposite from their own. This is just an initial foray into the concept. Once thinkers can see the opposing side of an idea, then they can search the motivations, information, and influence that goes into that idea. Through discussion and looking at both sides, other motivations and possible positions are often brought to light. Seeing things from other perspectives aids learners in becoming more introspective and to more thoroughly understand their own ideas. It is important for each individual to understand what they think and, most importantly, why it is what they think. This is how we as teachers make great strides in teaching students how to think for themselves while at the same time teaching and discussing content.

In the pages that follow, you will find examples of what I call *Argument Aids*. Some may call them worksheets, but I call them scaffolds. They are not meant to take the place of instruction in any way. Instead, these are designed to help students work their way through each stage of argument as they progress towards independence within the concept. Each scaffold can be customized to fit specific situations and tailored to where students are in their mastery. Most scenarios where I use these with students involve me adding or subtracting words, phrases, and the like in order for students to understand that their thinking in each case should focus on specific knowledge and understanding goals.

The first thing that students will need to do when composing an argument is to perform preliminary research. This is not thorough and comprehensive research as that will come later in the process. However, some reading or other research to get an introduction to the topic at hand is necessary. Often times in the classroom this will take the form of some sort of direct instruction or reading assignments from the teacher as background knowledge. I find the first time working with argumentation is made exponentially more effective if students work with a topic that they have already been taught or in which they are well versed.

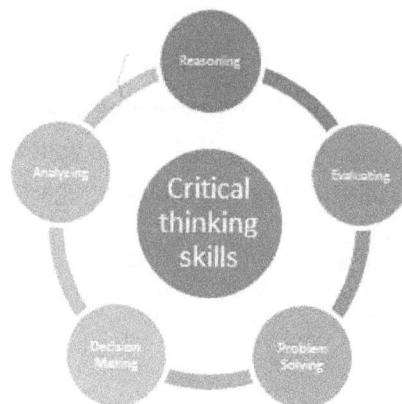

Constructing a Claim

What Ideas or position have you developed through your preliminary experience or research?

```
[                                                                    ]
```

Is there likely to be sufficient evidence, theory, fact, or interpretable data to support your claim? List some resources.

```
[                                                                    ]
```

Are there claims that may be similar to or opposite of your ideas that have been made previously? Describe them.

```
[                                                                    ]
```

Once you have determined that your ideas are different from those that have previously been argued, state your claim so that it is very clear and precise. Will people reading or listening to your claim be very clear about what you are saying? Have you been as specific as possible? Write your Claim as specific and precise as possible here. Be sure to use appropriate language and vocabulary regarding the subject matter at hand.

```
[                                                                    ]
```

Their confidence will be higher and the focus can remain on the process and thinking rather than on learning new material. As students increase their skill level, topics of which they have less background should be used until they get to a level of skill commiserate to a true critical thinker and can assess evidence and thoughts on topics of which they know little or nothing.

The "Constructing a Claim" scaffold is designed to help students work through the progression involved with creating a claim of their position or understanding and making that claim as precise, accurate, and original as possible. It makes clear that learners need to have done some preliminary reading or research in order to begin creating a claim. I always tell students that there is a possibility that their claim will change after they do more in-depth research, but there has to be a starting point that drives further research. When following the "Constructing a Claim" scaffold, the student is asked what constitutes their preliminary ideas. Students need to determine if there will be ample evidence to argue their point. Hopefully, during introductory research the student has found multiple sources of evidence that support their claim. I often remind students that this is likely the sort of evidence that led them to their claim in the first place. Next, students must determine if their ideas are similar to others' ideas that have already been written about or discussed. If their ideas are, then the student should reexamine their claim to see if they are repeating what someone else has done. If so then they should find a way to add to the argument by further detailing it or finding other evidence that can serve to further strengthen the claim and argument. Students should try and be innovative in some way. This may not always be possible, but the instructor should know which situation is which. Finally, the student must succinctly write their claim. It is important to use appropriate subject area vocabulary and to be clear about what they are saying. There is no place for vagueness in the area of the claim. Students should be encouraged, just like in any other essay, to be sure their topic is not too narrow to elaborate on and not too broad as to be overwhelming.

The scaffold can be modified to fit any particular situation. In a case where students might be researching a topic dealing with renewable energy sources or Green Energy, the first portion of the handout might be modified to look like the following:

Through your research of wind energy, hydroelectric energy, geothermal energy, solar energy, and nuclear energy, what ideas have you formed based upon their viability in your part of the Unites States?

In a situation where the topic could concern a science class or a particular scientific perspective, such as on the previous Green Energy question, the next portion might look something like this:

Is there likely to be sufficient scientific and research based evidence, scientific theory, common and/or current scientific understandings, or interpretable data to support your claim? List some resources. Give 2-3 sources from which you derived your ideas and that might be useful in your further understandings.

The amounts of modification and personalization possible are limitless.

Get Your Evidence Together

Facts from text or other print resources. Verifiable and trusted online information	Content Area Understandings or background information generally agreed upon in the field.

What Evidence or Data supports your Claim?

What ideas would you use to prove you are right?

Specific Examples Regarding the situation Specific Examples Similar to the situation	Expert Opinion or Information Experiences or Other Support

The *Argument Aid* that will support students next is the "Getting Your Evidence Together" organizer. Students can often confuse evidence itself with the reasoning used to connect the evidence to the claim. Often students include their reasoning, the "why" part of the argument, rather than the fact based evidence that supports their reasoning. In the scaffold here, students are prompted to deliver facts and other evidence only. They are not prompted to explain anything because that is done in the next steps. Here learners only look to see what is fact, expert opinion, accepted theory or ideology, examples that are the same or similar, and data/statistics. These are things that are not generally going to be disputed and that students can reason through or interpret to meet their needs in the argument.

Each section specifically asks for a certain type of fact or data. Often, students will latch onto one piece of evidence and attempt to form an entire argument around that idea. The scaffold here allows students to see that multiple pieces of evidence are necessary to formulate a strong argument. Many ideas and facts should go into the process of forming an opinion and a claim, thus there should be many ideas here as well. In this scaffold, learners also see that their evidence should come from different sources and from a variety of foundations. Students see that facts, expert opinions, understandings that are accepted in the field or content area, and situations or ideas that are similar to the subject of the argument are all appropriate places to search and locate evidence. The scaffold encourages variety, corroboration, and thoroughness in the hunt for evidentiary support.

The "Getting Your Evidence Together" scaffold can be tailored to fit content areas in general or specific cases or topics. An example of this might be a scenario where history students are researching the events

Information from your textbook, non-fiction texts from the "History" section of the media center, scholarly online journal article from Google Scholar, information from websites ending in: .edu, .gov, .org	Accepted interpretations of WWI and the US involvement, historical thinking and theories of the events leading up to US involvement in WWI. Understandings about the culture of the early 20th Century.

leading up to the U.S. entering World War I. The specific ideas students may be looking for and the places that they might trust to find those ideas are tailored specifically to the subject in this example.

In another example, students might be working to argue their

Ideas or interpretations from literary critics or experts on this and other poems by Frost Experience you have had with the subject of this poem	Examples similar in theme, use of literary device, or subject matter in other texts by Frost Examples similar in theme, use of literary device, or subject matter in other texts by other authors

specific interpretation of a poem they are reading by Robert Frost. The example shows how the scaffold can be modified to ask students to make connections across texts. This may include texts from other authors and also texts from Robert Frost that are similar in theme, use of literary device, or subject matter. Further, here the students are asked to seek expert interpretation and also to examine their own personal experiences with the subject matter. Overall, students seek information and ideas that they may not generally have sought out and thus they are beginning to think more critically about the subject matter.

Students can often find the evidence they need to support their arguments. Using these scaffolds, students have now been encouraged to find appropriate amounts of evidence. With that evidence must come a thorough explanation of how the evidence connects to the claim. This is where students often struggle. Frequently, learners write facts or other evidence and they see the connections in their mind but do not put it on paper. They essentially have evidence but leave the reasoning up to the reader. The "So What? Reason Through Your Evidence" scaffold helps to not only remind students to fully explain their evidence and the connections to the claim, but it helps them see those connections more clearly and therefore explain the connections more effectively in their writing. The scaffold is short and sweet but does several things to help writers. First, it reinforces the idea that they should be working with several pieces of evidence for their argument. In addition, students see that they should relate the connections between the evidence and the claim thoroughly. They should show how it is supportive and explain all of the connections. In addition, here students are asked to show why their sources are legitimate and why they should be trusted. This is also an often overlooked piece of

So What? Reason Through Your Evidentiary Support

Evidence/Data

How does this data/evidence support or prove your claim? What are all of the connections between your data/evidence and your claim?

Why is this evidence legitimate? Why should it be trusted? What understandings support the legitimacy of the evidence?

Evidence/Data

How does this data/evidence support or prove your claim? What are all of the connections between your data/evidence and your claim?

Why is this evidence legitimate? Why should it be trusted? What understandings support the legitimacy of the evidence?

Evidence/Data

How does this data/evidence support or prove your claim? What are all of the connections between your data/evidence and your claim?

Why is this evidence legitimate? Why should it be trusted? What understandings support the legitimacy of the evidence?

creating arguments. Readers need to know why they should believe the source of the evidence and what makes the source appropriate and an "expert" or "factual" source. Working through these reasoning areas will make students' arguments much stronger.

The scaffolds regarding claims and evidence can easily be modified to very specifically help students as they work completely and effectively through a topic. After they have decided on a claim and found the evidence that they need to support it, their focus is on more general concerns, such as those presented in the reasoning scaffold. The reasoning, counterclaim, and rebuttal *Argument Aids* are not conducive to this same customization because these parts of the argument depend heavily, if not completely, on the claim and evidence that arguers have chosen and researched. Teachers can work with students individually to help them work through these phases. Also, in the multiple stages of instruction, teachers can modify these scaffolds for the class to follow along as they create their model argument or as they examine an argument that has already been created. In the following example, the evidence scaffold has been modified in this way.

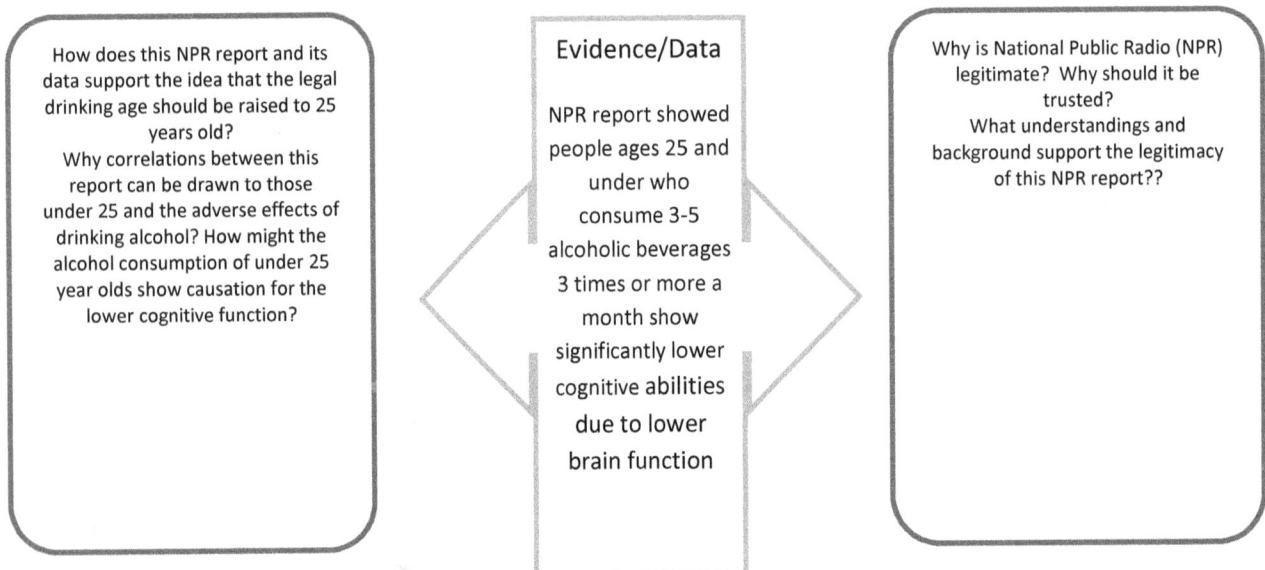

How does this NPR report and its data support the idea that the legal drinking age should be raised to 25 years old?
Why correlations between this report can be drawn to those under 25 and the adverse effects of drinking alcohol? How might the alcohol consumption of under 25 year olds show causation for the lower cognitive function?

Evidence/Data

NPR report showed people ages 25 and under who consume 3-5 alcoholic beverages 3 times or more a month show significantly lower cognitive abilities due to lower brain function

Why is National Public Radio (NPR) legitimate? Why should it be trusted?
What understandings and background support the legitimacy of this NPR report??

As can be seen, the idea of explaining fully the connections between the NPR report on cognitive function decline for consumers of alcohol under the age of 25 and the connection to the claim that the legal drinking age should be raised to 25 years old is explored for the students. Often in the beginning and in common arguments, students should be seeking correlation between events or logical lines of reasoning. These kinds of patterns of connection, correlation, and (hopefully) causation are basic logical reasoning patterns which students can be shown. A simple internet search turns up a multitude of examples of basic argumentative reasoning patterns which are sufficient to argue causation. For examples, I often have my students watch shows such as "Law & Order" or other constructive items about the law. Making these connections can be one of the most significant differences between an argument that is mediocre and one that is good or great. Fully detailing and thoroughly explaining the correlations, connections, and thus causation of the evidence is what leads students to convincing and superb arguments.

If students only complete the CER portion of these scaffolds they will have a mediocre argument. They will already have done more than many others as they will have provided the point of their writing, the evidence that supports their point, and they will have reasoned through, and thoroughly explained, both evidence and the reasons that the evidence supports their point. However, if learners are truly going to write the best possible arguments, then they will continue on to the more difficult, yet rewarding, parts of the argument. They will begin to look at the counterargument and the rebuttal. These have been touted by most students as the most difficult things to work through when writing arguments. Seeing things from other perspectives and alternative points of view can be difficult. The counterargument scaffold is titled "An Alternate Assessment of the Circumstances: The Counterargument."

An Alternate Assessment of the Circumstances: The Counterargument

The counterargument is an alternate claim along with the data/evidence and reasoning which attempts to explain the same thing that you are attempting to explain in a different way or from a different point of view. In order to fully solidify an argument, you must also examine alternate proposals or possibilities.

When you did your original research, examined evidence, and formulated your claim, what other possible explanations or ideas could you have supported that are somewhat different than what you chose? Brainstorm some of those ideas here.

Choose one idea that was different than yours, which has some support, and write a claim for that idea. This will be your counterclaim.

What is an alternate point of view to my claim? What claim can be made from this point of view that offers an alternate explanation/theory?	
What data/evidence is there which supports this alternate claim?	
What reasoning might connect the data/evidence to the alternate claim?	How is the data/evidence interpreted to support the claim?

Although it helps to see the different pieces of the counterargument, it is still difficult to teach the critical thinking necessary to actually determine what may constitute a counterargument. Here, students should review their original research and seek other ideas that they did not choose or alternative ideas that may have come across in their research. In the beginning, the teacher can provide a counterargument and have students complete the rest of the scaffold. Students can work their way up to the critical assessment of information and ideas that leads to this piece of argument. Once the counterclaim is found, the rest is somewhat easier. Students are essentially doing a miniature version of an argument to support the alternative claim. Evidence must be found in support of the counterclaim and reasoning for that evidence. Often that will come from the previous research. Once students have detailed the counterargument here, they can then move on to the rebuttal, which will negate the counterargument and should simultaneously add authority to the original claim, evidence, and reasoning described.

The counterargument scaffold can also be modified or partially created to help show students how to work through this more difficult piece of argument. In the example seen here, the original claim from an Oceanography class referenced the adverse effects of overfishing on coastal marine environments. Some of the evidence provided dealt with the decimation of specific fish populations. Also, evidence pointed towards declining tourism based on the loss of specific fish populations and subsequent economic issues therein. Using the scaffold this way allows the teacher to work with students as they learn to think in the specific way that we want them to think...critically. The critical thinking and assessment of ideas comes easier through this modeling.

An Alternate Assessment of the Circumstances: The Counterargument

The counterargument is an alternate claim along with the data/evidence and reasoning which attempts to explain the same thing that you are attempting to explain in a different way or from a different point of view. In order to fully solidify an argument, you must also examine alternate proposals or possibilities.

When you did your original research, examined evidence, and formulated your claim that overfishing was detrimental to the coastal habitat, what other possible explanations or ideas about overfishing could you have supported? Brainstorm some of those ideas here.

> *Overfishing brings money into the economy that would otherwise not enter.*
>
> *Overfishing is the only way that the coastal economy can survive in its current state.*

Choose one idea that was different than yours, which has some support, and

write a claim for that idea. This will be your counterclaim.

What is an alternate point of view to my claim?
What claim can be made from this point of view that offers an alternate explanation/theory?
The current economic benefit to the coastal community outweighs the possible ecological problems caused by overfishing.
Find the Data that supports the claim of the necessity of overfishing in some coastal economic areas. Look for evidence that shows the lack of other viable options and also evidence that suggests the ecological problems are not devastating to the ecosystem.

Connect the evidence you find supporting the claim fully to the idea that overfishing is necessary. Thoroughly explain why your data shows the negative effects on the economy that stopping overfishing would have.	Show correlation between your evidence and the idea that overfishing is necessary.
	Show a lack of correlation between overfishing and ecological problems in these areas.
	Shoe that if there is a correlation between ecological problems and overfishing it does not represent causation.

The Rebuttal: Controverting the Counterargument?

List a counterclaim different than the original claim

When you did your original research and created your claim, why did you not choose to

support this alternate idea?

What can you find wrong with the data/evidence, the legitimacy of that evidence, or the

reasoning used to connect the data/evidence to the counterclaim?

Data/Evidence	
Why is it not Legitimate?	Why is it not accurate or applicable?
What is the reasoning that connects this evidence to the claim or interprets the evidence to support the claim?	
What is an alternate way to see/interpret these connections that does not support the Counterargument?	

In the scaffold titled "The Rebuttal: Controverting the Counterargument" the process of negating the counterargument comes into clear focus for the learner. After writing the counterclaim first on the page, the learner should determine why they did not choose that as their claim. This will help them as they work through the rebuttal process. Next, the student follows the guidance of the scaffold in order to determine why the evidence supporting the counterargument is inadequate in some way. This can involve the legitimacy of the source, the interpretation of the data, the relationship of the data to the claim, the factual nature of the evidence, and a plethora of other reasons that the data is poor. The student then works through the reasoning that connects the evidence to the claim. This can be faulty or misinterpreted data, use of logical fallacies, use of poor reasoning in general, and many other inappropriate reasoning skills. Furthering their rebuttal, writers can examine the evidence and the counterclaim to look for other ways to interpret that evidence in which it does not effectively support the counter claim. They may even find ways in which it may support their original argument. Although not all of these are necessary, the more points of contention students make against the counterclaim and counterargument, the more significant their original argument becomes.

Once again, the rebuttal scaffold can be modified to fit the present situation and to help model for students how the thought processes of the rebuttal come to fruition during the argument. Once a counterargument has been chosen, it can be put into the scaffold to give students a starting point. Then, the rest of the sheet can be modified to walk learners through their thinking. In the example, we see a counterargument on the subject of the need for social promotion in schools states that social promotion is needed with evidence showing students who are retained exhibit a higher rate of dropping out. The scaffold can work to guide students through a rebuttal of this idea.

The Rebuttal: Controverting the Counterargument

List a counterclaim different than the original claim

Social Promotion is a more appropriate option for intervention with unsuccessful students in primary and secondary schools.

When you did your original research and created your claim, why did you not choose

to support this alternate idea?

What can you find wrong with the data/evidence, the legitimacy of that evidence, or

the reasoning used to connect the data/evidence to the counterclaim?

Data/Evidence	
Students who are retained one or more times in primary or secondary schools drop out of school before completion at significantly higher rates than students who are not retained.	
Why is it not Legitimate? Does the data on drop-out rates come from respectable data sources? If so it is legitimate and the rebuttal must come from another area.	Why is it not accurate or applicable? Does the drop-out data apply to this argument? If so then the rebuttal must come from another area.
What is the reasoning that connects this evidence to the claim or interprets the evidence to support the claim? The connection is one of correlation. The higher drop-out rates correlate with students who have also been retained in a grade at least once. The argumentative reasoning is that the retention causes the higher likelihood of dropping out of high school.	
What is an alternate way to see/interpret these connections that does not support the Counterargument? To rebut the reasoning here you must question the correlation and the likelihood of causation. Does the drop-out rate actually correlate with retention? If so examine the likelihood of causation. Is it clear that the retention is a cause of increased drop-out rates or is there a possibility that there is another cause that also correlates? Explore this idea.	

As can be seen, the rebuttal scaffold is more detailed in this methodology. Students must be guided through steps and this should be done as a class or in small groups. Some of the thinking is done for the students in order to lead them along the path, however the final determination of whether the correlation can be reasoned as causation is left up to the student. They have been pointed in the right direction and can now explore the options and critical thinking aspects on their own. The more practice students get at this kind of thinking the more they will become adept at it. The scaffold can be modified at different intervals and at varying levels of completion to slowly release the responsibility of thinking in this manner to the students.

The goal of this kind of teaching is critical thinking, critical assessment of information and ideas, as well as giving students the tools to monitor their learning and progress through metacognitive awareness. To accomplish this, there must also be help to guide their introspective and critical thinking. One of these such scaffolds is the "Eyewitness Account" sheet. Although it is not necessarily all about being an eyewitness, it does require students to see the subject matter from multiple perspectives. This *Argument Aid* is something like a checklist style of critical assessment of individual ideas and contributions to a subject matter. Students are pushed to truly examine the individual factors that can affect the opinions and ideas of others. Essentially, one must truly consider where ideas and information come from because even if one is working with accepted understandings from a content area or field of study, there are always multiple factors to be considered when deciding to trust a source, opinion, "fact," or first-hand account. These mental exercises work for scholastic endeavors and for real-life situations such as when students are watching the news, reading textbooks, doing outside reading, on the internet, in the library or in any scenario where they must determine the validity of information. These are true life skills.

Eyewitness Accounts

What event or idea might "witnesses" have perspective on? **Describe the "understandings" involved with the event or idea.**	**Witness:** **What might they:** **Think-** **See-** **Hear-** **Feel-** How are they similar to others- How are they different from others- What is their possible bias- What motivates this witness-
Who or what might be effected by this event or idea?	**Witness:** **What might they:** **Think-** **See-** **Hear-** **Feel-** How are they similar to others- How are they different from others- What is their possible bias- What motivates this witness-
When examining Perspective remember: **-Individual Experience** **-Individual and group bias** **-Cultural Norms** **-Motivation** **-Who benefits and why** **-How is this connected to other ideas** **-Political Affiliation** **-Economic Status** **-Powerful/Powerless** **-Voice – are they heard or silent** **-Education** **-Status in the Topic Area** **-Previous Actions** **-Who are they similar to** **-Who are they different from**	**Witness:** **What might they:** **Think-** **See-** **Hear-** **Feel-** How are they similar to others- How are they different from others- What is their possible bias- What motivates this witness-

As always, this can be modified to fit distinct content areas, situations, and assignments.

The argument chart is another graphic organizer that helps students get their argument together. It is simplistic as it has similar explanations and questions for students to ask themselves that have been found in some of the other scaffolds presented here. However, this is also something that can be modified for students to use when they are analyzing the arguments of others or examining arguments that teachers have given for learners to dissect. Thus, it is a good aid to students anytime they are working with arguments.

These scaffolds are designed to accompany activities centered on argumentation. In general, though, they are really tools that help to teach students how to critically assess their own ideas and the ideas of others. These activities were originally designed through work with science students in the realm of research and scientific argumentation. However, since that time, the activities presented here have been used in other science classes (such as astronomy, oceanography, physics, chemistry, and biology), English classes with much success, social science classes (such as history, geography, AP history, AP geography), and even geometry classes to help students learn to think. The unlimited potential for modification and application in individual content areas makes these scaffolds an invaluable tool for classroom teachers across all curricular areas. The ideas which have led to using Argumentation have been used by teachers for more than a thousand years. Aristotle, Socrates, and multitudes of other teachers have made use of these manners of intellectual activity involved in order to teach their students to think critically. We should be so fortunate as to continue this great line of teachers with similar and boundless success.

Part of Argument	Description	Questions to ask yourself	Your Argument
Claim/qualifiers	This is your argument. What are you trying to prove or convince someone of? Make this statement clear and precise.	What am I trying to prove? What am I saying is the correct answer or explanation? What am I saying is the right idea or interpretation?	
Data Evidence	This is the data that you are using to support your claim. This can also be referred to as the evidence that you have to show that your claim is correct or the right idea to consider	What facts did I consider when deciding on my claim? What evidence will convince others that I am right? What facts/evidence support my claim?	
Legitimacy	This is where you prove that your evidence should be trusted and is authentic. You must show your data/evidence to be from legitimate sources and factually based.	Why is this data/evidence assuredly facts that can be used in this specific field? Are my sources experts? Are my sources and facts accepted in the field I am examining?	
Reasoning	This is where you show why your data/evidence supports your claim. You are making the connections and showing why the evidence supports your thinking. You are thoroughly explaining how you determined your ideas based on the evidence you provided.	How does my evidence support my claim? What is the connection between my evidence and my claim? Why should my evidence be believed as support? What understandings support the connections that I have made between my evidence and my claim?	
Counterargument	This is where you think of positions or claims that others may have different from your argument. This is where you determine what someone who doesn't agree with you might believe. This is where you determine why others might have a different opinion	What is an alternate point of view to the subject matter? Why might someone believe an alternate point of view for the subject matter? What evidence might someone give to support an alternate claim?	
Rebuttal	This is how you convince others who hold opposing view that your view is correct. This is how you show that opposing points of view are invalid or incorrect. This is where you show why opposing evidence is invalid or does not support opposing claims	Why did I not choose this as my claim? Why is the counterclaim incorrect? What supports my claim as more valid or more reasonable than the counterclaim? Why is the evidence supporting the counterclaim incorrect? Why are the understandings supporting the counterclaim not effective?	

When you Argue...be A-BCERCR*

Argument made Simple

*BERSERKER –Norse Warrior

A- Audience

- When you write your audience is one of the most important things to consider.
- You must balance being clear enough in your explanations with treating your audience like they know more or less than they do...

B-Background

- You can't just jump into your argument.
- You must set the stage for where you are going.
- Why are you even examine this subject matter?
- What is the pertinent information the audience needs before you get started?
- Make sure the audience understands the context of the argument...

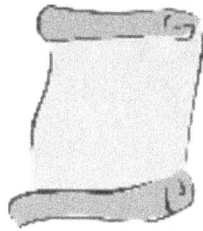

C-Claim

- This is your thesis statement.
- This is the point you are arguing.
- This is your position on the subject.
- This is what you are trying to convince the audience of.
- This is what you are saying is the answer.
- This statement should be clear and precise.

E-Evidence

- These are the facts that led you to your claim.
- This is the data or evidence you are using to prove your point.
- Be sure your evidence is acceptable in the content you are arguing in.
- Be sure you evidence comes from Legitimate sources in the content area you are working in.

R-Reasoning

- This is where you clearly show why your data/evidence supports your claim.
- You are making the connections obvious to the audience and showing why the evidence supports your thinking.
- What is the connection between my evidence and my claim?
- Show why should your evidence be believed as support for your claim?
- You should have at least twice as much reasoning as evidence.
- BE THOROUGH.
- Do the thinking for your audience

C-Counterargument

- This is where you think of positions or claims that others may have different from your ideas.
- This is an alternate explanation or idea.
- This is where you determine why others might have a different opinion.
- Here you make sure the audience understands that you have considered alternate ideas as you developed your own.
- This is where you think critically about your ideas.

R-Rebuttal

- This is how you convince others who hold alternate view that your view is correct.
- This is how you show that alternate points of view are invalid or incorrect.
- This is where you show why counterargument related evidence is invalid or does not support counterargument claims.
- This is where you show errors or fallacies in reasoning associated with alternate viewpoints.

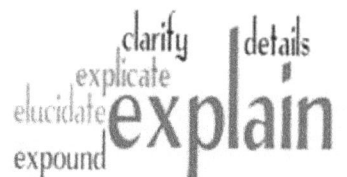

www.ingramcontent.com/pod-product-compliance
Lightning Source LLC
Chambersburg PA
CBHW080938040426
42443CB00015B/3471